How To Start a Consulting B

5 Steps to Get Your Business Up an...

Ever dreamed of owning your own consulting business, but you weren't sure where to start? If so, this is the book for you!

Author Armida Savage, one of Australia's most respected consultant, takes you through five steps to business success, from conceptualizing your business, to developing a detailed business plan, to launching. In this book, you'll learn how to evaluate your business idea, how to determine your pricing and calculate profitability, what technology systems to consider that will help you get ahead, and more. Whether you're just getting started or you need a little push in the right direction, this is your go-to guide for figuring out all the ins and outs of starting a consulting business.

About Armida Savage

When it comes to finding the perfect career in Australia, Armida is the go-to source. After all, she has over 13 years' experience recruiting for some of the top companies in the most competitive industries. Her experiences include connecting with candidates from across the globe while working with some of the most prominent multinational corporations to deliver high-quality recruitment and career coaching services.

With an emphasis on delivering a hands-on approach to recruitment, Armida established ARMIDA Consulting in 2017 with the mission of giving employers a more unique and efficient approach to recruitment. Her philosophy is a quality over quantity approach that emphasizes getting to know candidates. That includes spending a significant amount of time understanding candidate's goals and dreams, and working with them to improve their job-seeking skills. By matching candidates to their perfect career—and not just the perfect job—Armida helps organisations find the right skilled experts.

Armida's competitive advantage is that she genuinely cares about her clients and every candidate she meets. Whether it's understanding a company's resource requirements or a candidate's career aspirations, Armida works tirelessly to transform goals into realities.

To my family, thank you for your love and support.

How To Start a Consulting Business in Australia
5 Steps to Get Your Business Up and Running for Success!

Disclaimer

The material in this publication is of the nature of general comment only, and does not represent professional advice. It is not intended to provide specific guidance for particular circumstances and it should not be relied on as the basis for any decision to take action or not take action on any matter which it covers. Readers should obtain professional advice where appropriate, before making any such decision. To the maximum extent permitted by law, the author and publisher disclaim all responsibility and liability to any person, arising directly or indirectly from any person taking or not taking action based on the information in this publication.

Table of Contents

Introduction: Why Should You Start a Consulting Business?

My friend called me up the other week, looking for some advice on how to start a consulting business. We talked for some time, going over a number of aspects related to starting a business—the different legal structures, determining what services she'd offer, how to market the business, and more. After a fairly exhaustive session, she decided she wanted to digest all the information I had given her. But when we talked next, she mentioned that she was not in a rush to start a business and will revisit whether she should start up a business or not.

That's when I asked her the most important question again: "Why do you want to start this business?"

And that's the question anyone who is reading this book should be asking before going any further.

There are a number of reasons why someone might want to start a consulting business. While there are many reasons why someone might want to do this, it's important to find the personal reasons you want to do it.

For me, I got to a point in my career where I wasn't enjoying the work I was doing for other companies, mainly because their vision for delivering recruiting services didn't align with mine. They were all about the money; I was all about genuinely helping people. They were all about prioritizing work over personal life; I wanted to spend more time with my family. They expected me to do everything from new business to chasing invoices to training new employees, all while fulfilling my day-to-day job duties of finding stellar talent to fill roles at some of Australia's biggest corporations. I have always known that I would start my own consulting company one day and decided this was the year to start it.

And that's when Armida Consulting was born. In 2017, I quit my job to start my own company, to run things the way I felt they should be run, and continue to help businesses thrive by finding and hiring the best candidates. I've learned a lot over the years, and made my fair share of mistakes, including starting an online business that didn't work out. Based on those mistakes, I learnt what to do—and what not to do—and applied it when starting my current consulting business.

And that's why I wrote this book—to help others avoid some of the pitfalls of starting a consulting business.

Whatever your reason for starting a consulting business, my main message is this: Chase something you're truly passionate about. It's been my experience that pursuing passions is far more profitable than actually chasing money—and it's far more rewarding. Developing a business takes a lot of work, but when done properly, can be extremely satisfying and profitable.

What follows is a culmination of all my experiences starting and operating my own consultancy. I hope you find it useful as you seek out your own path forward.

Step 1:Evaluate Yourself

So, you want to start a consulting business? That's great! Before you dive in, though, it's essential to spending a little time evaluating your idea, your own core skills, and your reasons for starting a business.

Before doing any type of research, business planning, or taking the steps to legally form a business, it's important to determine that a consulting business is right for you. Ask yourself a few questions, and take some time to even write out the answers (I find writing things out helps me think through them). Ask yourself:

- Do I have the right entrepreneurial mindset?
- Am I self-motivated?
- What drives me?
- Do I have the skills/knowledge to generate new business?
- What is my appetite for risk?
- How comfortable are you with uncertainty?
- What are my own personal strengths and weaknesses?

If you're thinking about starting a business, you need to evaluate whether or not you're cut out for this. Most important in this process is to be honest with yourself. If you think deeply and objectively about these questions and find you're not fully comfortable with the responses, it might be better to not start a new business.

And that's ok! There's no shame in admitting this, but it's better to be honest with yourself at the outset than after a year or two of working on your business only to come up short.

But if you've thought about it and you're certain you've got what it takes, the only other thing to evaluate is why you want to start your business. Too often, people think starting their own business is going to skyrocket their annual earnings. While that's true in some cases, more often than not, hitting it big isn't something that comes quickly or easily—especially for consultants. Ask yourself why you want to start this business. Do you have a lot of domain expertise? Or are you looking to do something different? Are you looking for a way to be more creative? Do you have a unique idea or a concept that will help you run your business more effectively or efficiently than if you were working for someone else?

Whatever the case may be, understanding the "why" behind your desires to start a consulting business will inform almost everything you do once you actually get down to building it.

Step 2:Develop a Business Plan

A business plan is an essential document you will need to develop. It will be your roadmap to building your consultancy, and ultimately to your success. That said, keep in mind, things can change, and you'll need to be flexible when things don't go exactly according to plan.

It's wise to develop the business plan before you do anything else. The goal is to get as much of the details worked out before actually opening your doors.

There are several parts to a business plan, but the basic parts that every plan must include are:
- Business Summary
- Market Analysis
- Financials and Operating Budget
- Marketing Plan
- Exit strategy

Let's look at each of these in a little more detail.

Business Summary

Your business summary defines what your business will do, who you'll do it for, and how you'll do it. Write down what type of business you'll be, if you'll be specializing in a particular industry, and where you'll operate (locally, regionally, nationally, and globally).

It's also a good place to put your mission and vision statements. These two terms are frequently used interchangeably, but they're actually quite different. Your mission statement really answers the question of why you want to do what you do, whereas your vision statement describes your highest goal. Here are a couple of examples from my own business:

Mission Statement: ARMIDA Consulting's mission is to achieve the highest standards in the consulting practice of recruitment and professional services—to connect with people and be the destination of care and optimism.

*Vision Statement:*ARMIDA Consulting's vision is to be established as one of the leading recruitment and professional services company with a positive impact in areas of expertise. ARMIDA Consulting is also committed to the pursuit of innovation and to be known as the firm where personal attention will never become obsolete.

You may also want to take some time to work out what your core business values are. These are essential to developing a brand that your target customers will identify with and trust. Here are the values I developed when creating ARMIDA Consulting:

Collaboration – ARMIDA Consulting provides clients and candidates with the best service in terms of quality, innovation, and added value. We also aim to establish partnerships with clients focused on business sustainability and mutual growth.

Care – ARMIDA Consulting treasures long-term business relationships and genuinely cares for both clients and candidates. We are committed to the relentless pursuit of excellence in customer care and services, where personal attention will never become obsolete.

Integrity & Trust – We build transparent communication among all parties and provide the truth about all matters relating to their business. ARMIDA Consulting believes integrity and trust fosters longevity and generates positive energy.

Innovation – ARMIDA Consulting uses an efficient, streamlined process to collaborate with clients and candidates. We operate using an innovative strategy and cutting edge technology, which ensures both timely and successful placements. ARMIDA Consulting understands the fast paced nature of the workforce, and innovation is therefore at the forefront of our business.

These core values will be your guiding principles in everything you do.

Define Core Services

It's essential to clearly define what your services will be, so that potential clients will know what you do and what you *don't* do. For example, let's say you are starting a marketing consulting business. You have a lot of experience in social media marketing, content marketing, and website development. But you have very little experience in print advertising. Defining your core services provides potential clients with an idea of what you can do for them, while also allowing you to disqualify potential clients who want a different type of service.

Keep in mind that the goal here is twofold:
- To clearly communicate what you do.
- To make your services "buyable" at a variety of levels and price points (see the section below for guidance on pricing)

Lastly, clearly defining your services helps you to organise content on your website, which in turn will help website visitors find the information they want faster. For example, on my website, I have services for companies that need help recruiting, but also services for people who need career coaching. These are two separate pages, and both companies and individuals can easily get the information they're looking for without having to read through information that's irrelevant to them.

Market Analysis

It is essential to understand the market you'll be operating in and your position in the marketplace. This goes for both the industry you'll be serving as well as any competitors.

A good place to start is to describe the overall market conditions, as well as the industry you're going to serve. This can be general to start with, but it'll give you a good sense of how easy or difficult it will be to break into the market. For example, you might be looking to do consulting for a niche industry like waste removal or water treatment. While these might be large industries, there are likely only a handful of players in those fields. You will obviously need a high level of subject matter expertise if you expect to do consulting work for these companies and/or governmental bodies. With so few potential clients, competition to consult for them might be quite challenging. Compare that to, say, educational institutions. There are many, educational institutions out there, which might make it easier to win clients early and quickly.

Some information you should consider researching include:
- Overall industry size in terms of:
  - Dollar value
  - Number of companies in the industry
  - Industry growth rate
- What types of businesses are in the industry, segmented by
  - Size
  - Location
  - Market value

At this stage, it's a good idea to start formulating who your target customer is. Do individuals need your expertise? Or is it big businesses with a market value of $10+ million? Or is it small businesses with less than 10 employees? Maybe it's companies that offer a specific type of product or service, and your service complements theirs. Maybe it's government agencies or non-for-profits? Whatever the case may be, spend some time to think critically about who you really want to target.

Competitors

It's essential to know who your competition is and their position in the marketplace. Not only will this help you determine what your own position should be, but it can also help you understand what you'll be up against in terms of winning clients. How do you identify competitors? Well, if you have some industry experience, you possibly already have a few in mind. You can also always google "consultant" and your industry domain (tech recruiting consultant, for example). Other sources include business directories, industry association membership directories, or even your local or regional chamber of commerce.

There are some basic facts about your competitors that you'll want to identify, including:

- Company value
- Company size (number of employees, if applicable)
- Number of locations
- Types of services provided
- Areas of expertise
- Pricing (if available)
- Independent review scores (if available)

You may also want to chart out their social media presences and what type of content they create and share. This will come in handy when you develop and execute your marketing plan.

Now, you don't necessarily need to include every single competitor you find. Otherwise, you could be researching competitors from now until the end of time. I recommend focusing on the top five who will most likely be your most direct competition.

Market Need

Another important piece of information that will inform your approach and positioning is a description of the market need your business seeks to fill. For example, I frequently work with firms to fill technology roles, particularly at the managerial and higher levels. At any given time, there are a large number of tech jobs that need to be filled, but there are often not enough qualified candidates to fill them. Thus, there is a strong market need for qualified, high-level tech experts, and I work to fill that need through my own extensive network and methods for evaluating and matching candidates to positions.

This section can also point out a market need that your competitors may be overlooking or underserving. If that's the case, it's important to clearly state what the need is, why it's being overlooked, and how you intend to fill it.

SWOT Analysis

Once you've gathered a decent amount of market information, it's time to do a SWOT analysis. This is a handy tool to help you think critically about what sets your business apart.

SWOT stands for Strengths, Weaknesses, Opportunities, and Threats. The first two parts look internally at your prospective business, while the second two parts look at external factors that will affect your business. A common way to organize this information is in a grid, like this:

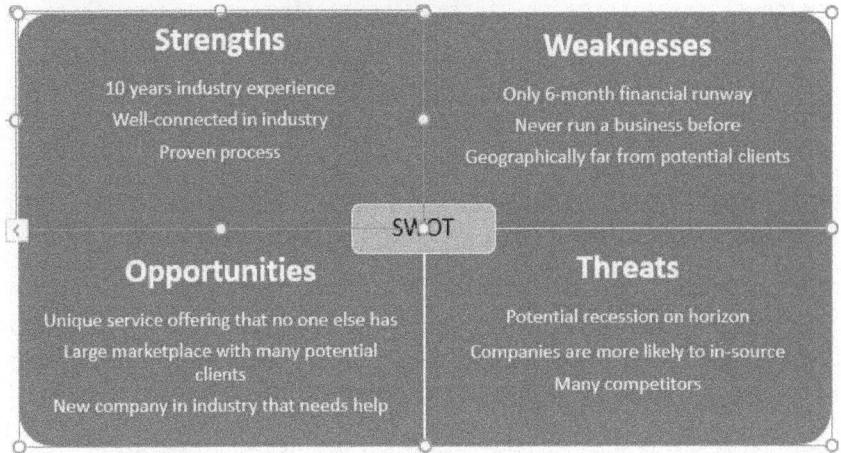

Strengths	Weaknesses
10 years industry experience	Only 6-month financial runway
Well-connected in industry	Never run a business before
Proven process	Geographically far from potential clients

SWOT

Opportunities	Threats
Unique service offering that no one else has	Potential recession on horizon
Large marketplace with many potential clients	Companies are more likely to in-source
New company in industry that needs help	Many competitors

I've listed three points under each category, but feel free to list as many as you can think of.

Financials and Operating Budget

As much as we like to think of the softer, more idealistic aspects of running a business, it's always good to remember that a business also needs to make money. And that can only happen if:
- You have paying clients
- You spend less than what you make

Your business operating budget will show how much you expect to make, and how much you expend to spend on expenses.

But before you do that, you need to figure out a few things. First, you need to figure out what your pricing structure is going to be. Are you going to charge per hour, per project, on commission, or some sort of hybrid model? How much are you going to charge? Will you have fixed prices, or will it be more of a sliding scale based on the scope of work? The answers to these questions will dictate your revenue model and profit margin.

If you already have considerable experience in your industry, you might have an idea of what to charge and what clients are willing to pay. If not, you may want to start with a realistic salary you'd like to earn and work backwards from there. For example, let's say you want to earn $100,000 before taxes. If you work a standard 40-hour work week, and you can bill for each of those hours, then you know you'll be able to bill 2,080 hours per year (40 hours/week X 52 weeks/year). That means you'll need to charge $48.07/hour ($100,000 ÷ 2,080 hours/year). We'll round that up to $50/hour.

However, you also need to take into account your expenses. Make a list of everything you think you'll need to spend money on in the coming year, along with the approximate cost of each item. These usually include (but aren't limited to):

- Equipment (laptop, printer, phone etc.)
- Office space
- Internet
- Mobile data
- Assemble Your Team – including Freelancer support (this is covered in the
- Marketing materials (business cards, website, etc.)
- Marketing expenses (advertising, content writing, etc.)
- Website hosting
- Professional association memberships
- Gas or other travel expenses (if you intend to visit clients in person)
- Entertainment (if you think you'll ever take clients out to lunch)

- Insurance
- Software licenses

Of course, the cost of some of these might be difficult to estimate. Don't worry about being exact at this point, but do be sure to include everything you think you'll need to spend money on.

Now, let's say your total annual expenses comes to $30,000. That means you'll need to gross $130,000 per year total. That brings your total billable rate to $62.50 ($130,000 ÷ 2,080 hours/year). Seems rather low for the amount of effort, right?

Well, one thing to take into account is that even if you work 40 hours/week, you likely won't be *billing* for each of those hours. You need to take into account time spent doing non-billable activities, such as marketing, researching and contacting prospective clients, meeting with prospective clients, going to industry and networking events, managing your team, etc. The truth is that you will never be only doing billable work. Even if you are able to bill 40 hours/week, you'll likely end up working 60-80 hours total. Why? Because you will *always need to be looking for new clients.* What's more, you may or may not have clients right out of the gate when you open, which means you'll need to work up to that level.

So, in order to account for non-billable time, I recommend you make your base hourly rate anywhere from 2-3 times the base. This might vary based on the industry you serve, your location, and other factors, but this should give you a good basis to at least estimate what you can expect to earn.

Lastly, you need to consider what the market is able to support. One of the goals of conducting market research is identifying needs for specific services—and what clients are willing to pay for them. Many firms might need a consultant with your particular skillset, but not everyone will be willing to pay for them. While we'd all like to be well-paid for our time and skills, there are limitations on what the market will support. Conversely, if you price your services too low, you could be winning more work than you can reasonably manage.

Once you've figured out what your pricing structure will be, you'll want to put all of these into a single budget with income in one column and expenses in another, and calculate your potential net profits. Once you do that, you can also forecast out the next 2 years. This is important to do so you can have an expectation about earnings. But be conservative! There's nothing that feels more deflating that giving yourself unrealistic expectations that will never come to fruition.

In addition to your forecasted budget, it's also imperative to put together a budget to cover your startup costs. This might include buying new equipment, putting money down on a leased office space, printing business cards, website hosting for your website, freelancers to help you with development, marketing, etc. It's smart to be as exhaustive and realistic as possible to ensure you have a good handle on your initial capital costs. This will be important should you require financing, as a small business bank loan might be necessary to cover your initial costs (see *Set Up Banking and Insurance* below).

One last note: When you first start out, it might be a good idea to pay yourself a lower salary than what you'd like, and reinvest some of your profits into the business. When you start a business, there's all kinds of expenses that are important to spend money on—a website, marketing collateral, etc. It's easier to pay for these from revenue rather than taking a loan (though you might need to do that as well, depending on your business model). And that means you take a lower salary to start. But don't worry, these are important investments that you're making that will (ideally) pay dividends for years to come. Additionally, it's a good idea to put some of your revenue aside in a rainy day fund. You never know what the economy is going to do, and having some extra cash on hand can be a lifesaver if you go through any rough patches.

Revenue and Profitability Forecast

Once you've developed your budget, it's time to build a revenue and profitability forecast. If you've done your homework and have an idea of what you're going to charge, and what your target is, you can break that down to the number of clients and/or projects you will need to secure and how much revenue you can expect to generate each month.

It's also a good idea to also look at your business from a profitability standpoint and not just sheer revenue. Revenue figures alone don't tell you if you're making money. Gross Profit is the money you make after you subtract all your expenses but before you pay taxes. You want to also calculate not only your profit, but your profit margin as well, expressed as a percentage. While there are a number of ways to calculate profit margin (and different types of profit margin), the simplest is *gross profit margin*, calculated as:

((Revenue – Expenses) ÷ Revenue) x 100 = %

For example, let's say your annual revenue is $100,000 and your operating expenses are $25,000. Your formula would look like this:

(($100,000 - $25,000) ÷ $100,000) x 100 = 75%

You would have a 75% profit margin. If you have access to the information, it might be helpful to ask other consultants in your industry what their profit margin is. Try to get an average profit margin, as that can vary from business to business. If your projected profit margin is much lower or higher than the average, you might be overlooking something in your business plan. It also gives you something to shoot for!

Start off by forecasting the first two years (or three), but I don't recommend forecasting more than that, as a lot of things can change. Keep in mind that you'll likely have larger and more expenses when you launch your business, particularly if you need to invest in equipment. Your forecast might look something like this:

Month	Month 1	Month 2	Month 3	Month 4
Revenue	$3,000	$4,000	$4,000	$5,000
Expenses	$3,000	$2,000	$1,500	$2,000
Profit	$0	$2,000	$2,500	$3,000
Profit Margin	0%	50%	62.50%	60%

Marketing Plan

A key part of running a consulting business (or any business for that matter) is to understand that *you always need to be searching for new clients*. This is a never-ending task, but one that will fuel your success in the long-run. And in order to be successful, you need to market your business—which means you need a marketing plan.

A marketing plan is like a mini-business plan within your business plan. It outlines who you're targeting, how you'll win their attention and attract them, and convert them into paying clients. As such, you'll want to include sub-sections in your marketing plan that addresses all of these aspects of marketing, as well as a way to measure.

So, what will specific actions and items you include in your marketing plan?

It's always good to start with your target. Build an ideal customer profile that includes the type of business you're targeting, as well as a customer "persona" that addresses more the individuals you want to speak to; i.e. manager, director, owner, etc. Focus on what their needs and challenges are, what they like and dislike, and where they get their information or turn to for help.

Next, think about where these businesses and individuals get information. That could be a long list, including trade publications, websites, trade shows, events, social media, etc. These are what can be called channels. Prioritize the channels from easiest to find and contact to most difficult. This is likely the best way to organize your marketing initially, as you will have a limited time and budget to devote to marketing. Taking this approach will help you focus on the easiest, fastest methods for reaching and converting prospects.

After that, map out your sales funnel, describing how a person moves from becoming aware of your business to actually buying. A typical sales funnel looks like this, though yours might be slightly different:

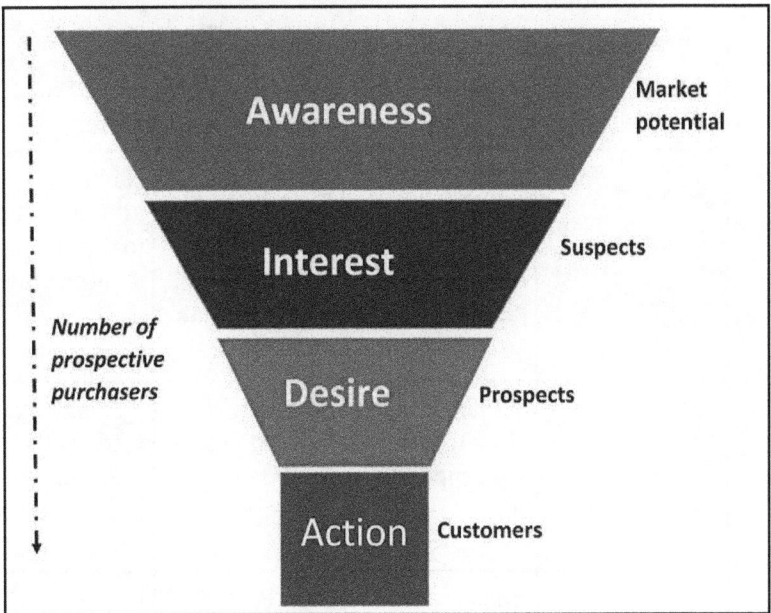

Image source: https://commons.wikimedia.org/wiki/File:The_Purchase_Funnel.jpg

For each stage, come up with 3-5 things you can do to move customers to the next level. These are your marketing tactics For example, your awareness stage might include speaking at industry events, posting LinkedIn content relevant to your industry, and using industry-specific hashtags on Twitter or Facebook. It's important to note that today's marketing is largely focused around content, but there are certainly other tactics that are more traditional, such as taking out an ad in an industry trade publication. For the purposes of your business plan, I recommend first focusing on tactics that you can do (or hire someone to do for you at a reasonable price), with material that is easily adaptable to other channels.

Once you have all your channels and tactics down, come up with a thematic calendar. I suggest dividing this up first into quarters with each quarter with a different theme relevant to your industry. Then, divide the quarters in months and insert a tactic or two for each level of the sales funnel under each month. When completed, your marketing calendar should look something like this:

THEME	Keeping the Tech Talent Pipeline Full		
MONTH	January	February	March
Awareness	5 Facebook posts with helpful tips for keeping the pipeline full	Networking event presentation: How to build your candidate database	LinkedIn article: 5 things to do right now to attract talent
Interest	Whitepaper: How to keep your pipeline full	Webinar: How to build your candidate database	5 Facebook feeds with relevant industry trends
Desire	Email newsletter: Recent placements and successes	Blog Post: How to Win in Today's Job Market	Email newsletter: How to Win in Today's Job Market
Action	For interested prospects, offer a 10% off deal if they begin by a certain date.	For prospects: Offer 5% off promotion	For prospects: Offer refer a friend promotion

One thing you'll notice is that some of the tactics might repeat themselves, but on different channels or through different media. The great thing about marketing today is that you can reuse marketing content across channels. Maybe you gave a great presentation to your local chapter of an important industry associat ion. You can use that material in a blog post, or on LinkedIn, etc. The key is determining what your audiences are interested in, and then creating content that will speak to those needs.

Exit Strategy

You may not want to work on your business forever, and if that's the case, it's a good idea to develop an exit strategy. You may also want to develop an exit strategy in case you learn that being independent isn't your thing, and you want to transition away from operating a business.

This certainly is an optional part of your business plan, but it might also be an essential one based on your personal goals for your business and your life. That said, it may also drive certain activities or approaches as you grow your business.

Your exit strategy will describe how you want to extricate yourself from your business. That might be as simple as shutting down and notifying any existing clients, but it might also require that you sell your client portfolio to another business or colleague. Think about what your goals are outside of the business, for example, you might want to retire early and buy a beach house. Knowing what your long-term goal is and how you will wind down your business will help you stay focused on the most important aspects of growing and operating your consultancy.

If you go through all of the above steps, you'll soon have a well-thought out business plan that you can use as a springboard and a roadmap to launching your own consultancy. One last note on this subject: Keep in mind that your business plan should be flexible. Market conditions change, clients want more (or less) work, you experience some life-altering event. Whatever the case may be, your business plan is not set in stone, and you should keep an open and flexible mind as things progress. It's always a good idea to revisit your plan regularly and adjust it as things in your life change.

Step 3: Finalize Your Business Details

If you've made it this far, congrats! You're almost ready to launch your consulting business. There are just a few important details that need to be worked out, many of which will shape the success of your new endeavor.

Assemble Your Team

Whether you're working by yourself or with others, you're going to need a team of experts who can support your business. These typically include:

- An accountant
- A lawyer
- A business development expert
- A graphic designer and/or website designer
- A content writer
- A marketing expert

Each of these professionals play an important role in launching and growing your business. Now, do you need all of them to work for you full-time right away? No, of course not! You'll likely need an accountant and lawyer up front, to help you get all the business structure and legal matters squared away so you can launch.

As for other four roles, you may be able to do them yourself. Think very deeply, though, about where your strengths and weaknesses are. Are you good at writing? Can you make cold calls to prospective clients? Are you adept at managing social media? I'm not suggesting you take on all the roles—after all, there's only so many hours in a day and you need to both build the business and serve clients as well. You need to stay sane and avoid burn out—a common challenge for entrepreneurs. Oftentimes hiring a team of experts can help you get ahead faster and allow you to concentrate on other areas of your business that are crucial to your success.

Choose a Business Structure and Register Your business

There are four basic business structures in Australia. They

are:

1. Sole Trader:Best for small businesses like a consultancy, Sole Trader businesses are the fastest and least expensive business class. The owner has direct control over the business and can claim all the profits. At the same time, the owner is also fully liable for any damages.

2. Partnership:As the name implies, this is when two or more people own a business. The partners share everything—from profits to liabilities. There are some tax advantages here, and a partnership agreement should be in place to clearly define how profits are paid out to each partner.

3. Company (Pty ltd):A company can be public or private, and is owned by shareholders, who appoint directors to run the company. Although liability is limited to company assets, but this structure is far more complex and expensive to set up and maintain than the previous two types.

4. Trust:A trust is where a business is managed by a third party, which then distributes income to its beneficiaries. Trusts are often used to hold property, and can also require a significant amount of administration and bureaucracy.

Depending on your situation, any of these types of businesses may be best for you. It's important to consult with your accountant to determine which will be best for you.

Develop a Business Name & Brand Identity

Your business name and brand identity are essential components to your business. They should capture your values and be instantly recognizable. Oftentimes, consultancies will take the name of their founder (e.g. ARMIDA Consulting—my name is Armida), but you certainly can choose any name that you feel fits your brand.

Once you choose a name, you need to register it, which can be done with the Australian Securities and Investments

Commission (ASIC, https://asic.gov.au). Keep in mind that you can only register a business name *that hasn't already been taken*. Luckily, ASIC has a business name search engine you can use to find out if the name you want is already taken.

Your brand identity is also an important part creating your business. While most people think of brand identities as just a logo, they're really far more involved. A brand identity includes your logo, a brand color scheme, a brand font, and a general visual look for all your marketing materials. This will serve to inform all collateral you create going forward, including business cards to your website to client proposals. Your brand identity must be unique and memorable, and this is a great time to engage a graphic designer, who can work with you to bring your vision to life.

Once you have a registered business name and brand identity you can do the following:

- Secure website hosting and build a website.
- Set up your email address
- Create any marketing materials you might need (business cards, brochure, prospectus, proposal template, etc.).
- Create your social media presences (LinkedIn, Facebook, Instagram, etc.). Keep in mind you don't have to be on every single platform. Figure out what your industry uses most and invest time and energy there.

Set Up Banking and Insurance
Once you've registered your business, you can also set up your business banking. If you don't have a lot of money saved up to support you in the early days of your business (before you win enough clients to support yourself), you may want to talk to banks about financing options. Many banks offer new businesses small unsecured loans that have low interest rates and/or low monthly fees. Getting some cash up front to pay your operating expenses will be a huge help as you start to develop your clientele.

You should also look into obtaining insurance, including professional indemnity, public liability, and business contents insurance (for property). For cents on the dollar, this will protect you and your business against any personal injury, property damage, or financial loss that might occur while you operate your business. It'd be terribly unfortunate for something to happen that causes a lawsuit, and the next thing you know you're out of business and maybe even a home!

Additionally, there are some insurances that are required for you to operate in certain parts of Australia. WorkCover or worker's compensation insurance is compulsory in every Australian state and territory, for example. WorkCover insurance covers the costs if an employee is injured or becomes ill because of their work. Luckily, when you're starting out, the costs are generally very low, as you likely won't be hiring many employees at the start. That said, there are large penalties for not being in compliance, and these could be so severe that you're unable to operate as a business.

Secure License and Permits

Some industries require you to have a license and permits to operate. This is customary for industries that are heavily regulated, but new government regulations are requiring more and more industries to obtain licenses and permits. Be sure to check out *https://www.business.gov.au* to see if you need a license and permit for your consultancy.

Fine Tune Your New Business Development Approach (or Find Someone to Do It for You)

The key to any successful business is acquiring new customers and retaining them. If you can't generate new business, you won't have a business for very long (even if you have one big, long-term client). You may or may not have significant business development experience, but if you don't you're either going to have to learn how to do it or find someone experienced who can do it for you.

There are a number of ways to generate new clients, but there are two methods I've found to be particularly useful. These are networking and cold calling (or emailing). Networking typically means going to industry events to meet people, but it could also include sporting events, volunteering, or even arranging a meeting with someone just to introduce yourself and your business. It's a great way to develop and nurture lasting business relationships with prospective clients, potential referral sources, or even future employees. Set a goal for yourself to go to a certain number of events each month and meet a certain number of people. Remember, though, that networking is about connecting with business people and learning more about them and their organisation.

In terms of cold calling and emails, you have to remember that it's purely a numbers game. The more people you reach out to, the more likely you will find someone who says yes. How do you know who to reach out to? Well, in order to do cold calling and emailing, you need to do prospecting first. That means spending time researching potential clients. This is where hiring someone to help you can come in handy, as prospecting can be a very time consuming process.

In fact, if you're not comfortable with these activities, it could be worthwhile to hire someone to do new business development for you. The key is finding someone you can trust, with a proven track record. That can be challenging, so make sure you take the time to fully vet anyone before hiring them, including checking their references.

Develop Your Terms and Conditions
All work you do for a company should be done under a contract. Some clients may have a contract for you to sign already, but you should also develop your own. Your contract needs to clearly state your terms and conditions of how you work, where you work, and how and when you'll be paid. It should also include your pricing structure, so it's clear how much a client will pay and the conditions under which charges may increase (out of scope work, late fees for nonpayment, etc.). It's a good idea to have a lawyer review your business contract first before you send it to any potential clients.

Step 4:Choose Your Technology

Technology is a key part of any business these days, even a one-person consultancy. In fact, technological improvements that enable us to work anytime from any location is partially what has made it possible for more and more people to break out on their own.

In addition to your laptop, phone, and internet connection, there are a handful of key technologies that you will likely need in order to succeed. There is a wide variety of software out there that will make your life infinitely easier as you launch your business. Here are a few to consider.

Website Content Management System (WCMS)

A WCMS enables you to make edits to your website, typically without having to know how to code. You may also often use a WCMS to produce blog posts, generate landing pages for specific services, and more. There are a number of free or inexpensive ones out there, but check with your website hosting company to see if they offer any specific tools or deals. A website designer will also likely be able to give you a recommendation or two, and can design a site specifically for a CMS.

Document Management

Depending on the nature of your consultancy, you may need a flexible document management system that enables you to store, organize, and share documents quickly and easily. This will be like your business' filing cabinet, and so security should be a high priority. Additionally, many services include (or offer) backup services. This is an essential feature that can really save you in case something happens to your laptop.

Office Document Suite

You will likely need software to produce documents, spreadsheets, presentations, and more. To do that, you obviously will need software (if you don't have it already). If you've spent any time in business, you know Microsoft is the most popular office software in the world, but there are plenty of alternatives (some that are even free).

Invoice and Accounting

You need a way to invoice your clients. Now, you could just send them a printed one in the mail, but this is the 21st century. Most businesses use some form of electronic accounts payable system to track and pay incoming invoices. The good news is that there are plenty of options out there, some of which are designed specifically for small businesses and independent consultants.

You want to be able to create and email invoices, but it's also a good idea to have a way to accept electronic payments. Some invoicing systems connect with a credit card payment gateway, which enables your clients to pay invoices by credit card. There are fees associated with this facility, but the convenience of it likely pays off. Additionally, you want to have a way to track expenses and determine profitability. Sometimes that's a matter of importing expenses from your bank or business credit card account; but sometimes you might need to keep track of receipts (this is particularly true if you're buying equipment that has a warranty).

Ideally, I recommend looking for a system that can handle both invoicing, payments, and accounting all in one.

Customer Relationship Management (CRM)

A CRM is a database that helps you keep track of leads and clients. If you're doing a lot of prospecting and cold calling, then a CRM will be a highly useful tool. There a lot of platforms out there, some of which are low-cost or free. The main thing to know here is that you need a system that is easy to input leads, and that can help you track the status of leads.

Applicant Tracking System

This one is helpful for businesses looking to hire employees and want to automate and streamline their entire hiring process. An applicant tracking system helps employers keep all their resumes in one place and provides you with the tools you need to build a talent pool, organise and track applicants. This is particularly useful when you're trying to fill multiple positions simultaneously, as it can ensure you focus your energy and time on the top prospects for a job.

Social Media Management

If you're handling all your business' online marketing, then a social media management platform can be a real help. There are a wide variety of tools out there, some which can handle multiple platforms and account simultaneously. It's best to know which social media networks you'll be spending the most time in, and then looking for a platform that can manage them all. You'll also want to look into a platform that offers analytics so that you can finely tune your messages and posts.

Step 5:Launch!

Now that you've crossed all your t's, dotted all your i's, filled out all your paperwork, and set up everything, it's time to launch your business! There are a lot of fun and creative ways to launch a business, but at the very least, it's a perfect opportunity to reach out to new prospective clients.

You might consider holding a formal launch event, where you invite peers, prospective clients, local business media, and other people you're already connected to. This could include hiring a venue, getting some light snacks and drinks, maybe even a DJ or some other form of entertainment. Or you can launch your business via social media channels by developing content and saying you are officially open. It's essential to have creative, high-quality marketing content for your target audience, be it blog posts, video, podcasts, or other format.

Additionally, it might be a good time to reach out to your local business media to introduce yourself. It's not uncommon to for them to profile local business owners, and the publicity can give you some much-needed visibility that boosts interest in your services early on.

Whatever approach you take, I highly recommend doing *something* to let people know you're in business. After all, businesses don't build themselves. They're built with hard work and persistence, and often a little luck.